The Dream Come True

The Story of Prophet Joseph
(Peace be upon him)

UK ISLAMIC ACADEMY

ISBN 978 1 872531 04 5

(*A free adaptation from Maulana Abul Hasan Ali Nadwi's writings*)

General editor: Iqbal Ahmad Azami

Language editor: Jamil Qureishi

Published by

UK Islamic Academy
P.O. Box 6645
Leicester LE5 5WT
United Kingdom

Website: www.ukiabooks.com

E-mail: info@ukiabooks.com

British Library Cataloguing in Publication Data
A catalogue record for this book is available from the British Library

Cover design: Sultan Faruqi
Illustration: Aisha Abdur-Rahman

Printed & Bound in the E.U.

Contents

	page
Foreword	4
Introduction	5
1. A wonderful dream, and a wicked plot	7
2. Joseph is cast into the well	11
3. Joseph is found by merchants	15
4. A scandal against Joseph	19
5. Joseph explains the meaning of dreams	24
6. The threads are drawn together	29
7. Building for the great re-union	35
8. The re-union	43
9. The dream comes true	46

Foreword

In the Name of God, the Beneficent, the Merciful.

The Dream Come True is one of a series of stories on the lives of the great Prophets, upon whom be peace, intended for children of 8 to 12 years. From the moment God created the world He started to reveal His guidance for mankind through His Prophets. These books relate the Prophets' experiences as they struggled to persuade the erring peoples of their day to obey and worship the one and only God. Much that is of relevance today can be learnt from the way these men, specially chosen by God for their task, taught, guided and trained the miscreants.

The Dream Come True, in the English language, has been written for Muslim children growing up in an English-speaking country. This Prophet has been given the name he is known by, in English rather than his original Arabic name to avoid confusion. Parents and teachers, however, should ensure that the traditional Qur'anic name is also known.

Children living in a non-Muslim society are often denied their traditional Islamic family background where stories from the Holy Qur'an were frequently heard. Parents and teachers have a duty to make up for the shortcomings of living outside an Islamic environment. *The Dream Come True* is intended to help them in their task by strengthening children's awareness of the guidance provided by God's Prophets who all bore the same message for mankind: that there is no god but the One, True God.

My thanks are due to Bro. Jamil Qureshi, Sis. Maryam Davies, my daughter Shifa' and my other children for their help in producing this book. May God bless them all and accept this humble effort and make it beneficial to all.

Iqbal Ahmad Azami

Introduction

Men are different from each other, and women are different from each other. They are stronger and weaker in different ways, and in this life, some have a higher, some a lower standing. But in God's eyes these differences are not important. When, in the life to come, God prefers one person above another, it is not because he or she is taller or richer or cleverer or better-looking. If God prefers one person above another, it is because he or she is stronger in prayer, stronger in remembering God.

Out of all mankind, the best of people were God's Messengers, His Prophets. He chose them as Prophets, because He had weighed their souls to the very last grain and, to the very last grain, found their prayer to be perfect. They remembered God always, both in the day and in the night. In defeat or failure, in the face of the mockery of others, in the middle of any danger to themselves, the Prophets were true to God, and spoke the truth. Likewise in the best of times, in victory and success, in gardens and palaces, in the love of their people, the Prophets were true to God, and spoke the truth.

In the same way, when the Prophets preferred one person above another, it was not because he or she was richer or cleverer or more beautiful, but because he or she was stronger in remembering God. What the Prophets desired was that those who followed in their line, those who came after them, should be God's true servants. To be a Prophet was a great blessing from God, and God's blessing on them was perfected when those who came after them were also like them in being true to God.

Abraham* was a Prophet, and God's true servant, and His friend. God perfected His blessing on Abraham, for after Abraham came Ishmael* and Isaac,* true servants of God and His Prophets. Then in the line of Isaac, came Jacob,* a Prophet also, and a true servant of God. Out of those who came from Jacob, God preferred Joseph,* (Yusuf, peace and blessings be upon him), who was His true servant and a true Prophet. Jacob also, and for the same reasons, preferred Joseph of all his eleven sons. In this story, which is one of the most beautiful of stories, you will understand why Joseph was chosen above the rest.

But why is it called the most beautiful of stories?

*Muslims are required to invoke Allah's blessings and peace upon the Prophets whenever their names are mentioned.

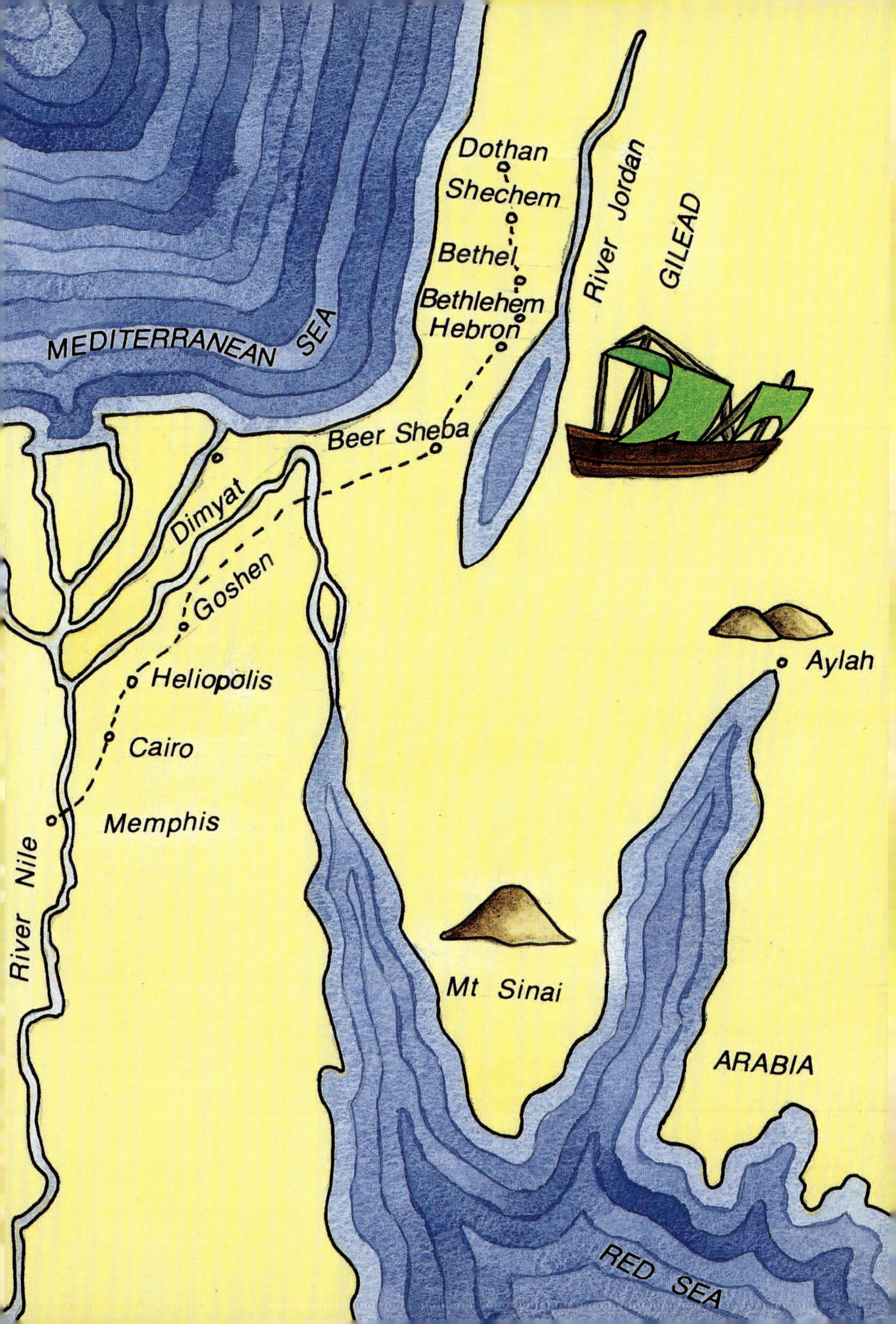
Dothan
Shechem
Bethel
Bethlehem
Hebron
River Jordan
GILEAD
MEDITERRANEAN SEA
Beer Sheba
Dimyat
Goshen
Heliopolis
Cairo
Memphis
River Nile
Aylah
Mt Sinai
ARABIA
RED SEA

1
A wonderful dream, and a wicked plot

Jacob was blessed with twelve sons. Joseph and Benjamin were the two youngest, and of the two, Joseph was older. The other ten had a different mother and were much older than Joseph and Benjamin.

Jacob loved all his sons but most especially he loved Joseph. Joseph was handsome, and his good looks were a test from God, a test for all those who saw him, and a test for Joseph himself. Though very young, Joseph was devoted in his prayers to God, and the very sight of him gladdened his father's heart. When Jacob saw Joseph, his face lit up with joy, and all the others saw that this was so. They saw that Jacob's heart went out to Joseph. Benjamin too loved Joseph; his heart was clear and innocent, and they were the closest of friends.

How Benjamin would miss Joseph, if ever Joseph went away! How Jacob would miss him, if ever the dearest of his sons went away!

Not so the ten older brothers. They would not miss Joseph. They were jealous of him. They said: 'Are we not stronger, do we not work harder? Why then is there such a light in our father's face when he sees Joseph?' But Jacob knew them in a way that they did not know themselves. Jacob knew of something in their hearts that they did not know themselves. These brothers did not ask: 'Which of us best remembers God?' Their hearts were not clear and not innocent, they had a grudge against Joseph.

One night, in a dream, Joseph saw eleven stars and the sun and the moon. In the dream, the stars and sun and moon bowed down before Joseph. Joseph told his father about this dream and asked him what it might mean.

Jacob thought for a long time before he answered. He said: 'It is a sign of God's favour to you. Your Lord will choose you and He will teach you how to understand the inner meaning of events. It is a sign that God will make perfect, through you, His blessings on my family, the family of Jacob, just as He did for the families of Abraham and Isaac, your great grand-fathers. As for why it will be so, and how it will be so, your Lord is surely the One who has Knowledge and Wisdom.'

Then, Jacob warned Joseph. He said: 'My son, do not tell your brothers of this dream. It may make them plot some harm against you.' It was not permitted to Jacob, a true believer and God's servant, to say anything against other people without clear proof. So Jacob did not say anything against his sons, Joseph's brothers. But he wanted to explain his warning to Joseph, so he added: 'Satan is a proven enemy of mankind.' Jacob was very afraid of what Satan might tempt Joseph's brothers to do.

Joseph was glad in his heart that God had chosen him, and he thanked God. His heart was clear and innocent, so his gladness showed in his face, and it showed in the lightness of his walk. His brothers saw this and followed him. Then they asked him what he was so glad about. When Joseph was silent, they said: 'We are your brothers. Surely you should trust us and be open with us.'

Joseph thought that what the brothers said was right. Because he wished only good for his brothers, he thought they must wish the same for him. So Joseph told them his dream.

The brothers pretended to be pleased for Joseph, but inside they burned with jealous anger. They said: 'We are a strong band, we ten, almost an army. Still, our father prefers Joseph and Benjamin. It is clearly unfair!' They thought that now, after Joseph's dream, it would be worse for them, that they would be thrown right out of favour. They plotted to do away with Joseph, to get rid of him somehow.

Certainly they knew that this was a terrible wrong to do. But they told themselves that it was the only bad thing they would ever do. They said: 'After that we will do only right actions, and be righteous people.' They thought about killing Joseph. But one of them said: 'No! Let us not kill him. Instead, we could throw him into some pit, and maybe some passing traveller will pull him out and take him far away!'

2
Joseph is cast into the well

The ten brothers asked Jacob to let them take Joseph with them on a short trip. When Jacob refused, they said: 'Father, what is wrong? Why is it that you do not trust us with Joseph? Surely we wish him well, truly we do. Let him come with us tomorrow, to play and pass the time. You can be sure we will be watching over him.' The brothers thought Jacob could not see through their smiles. They thought he could not see the jealousy in their hearts.

But Jacob could see it. He said: 'I am worried about letting you take Joseph. I am afraid that you may forget to watch over him, and in the meantime the wolves may snatch him away and eat him.'

The brothers laughed at the idea. 'What? We are a strong band, father, all but a small army. That being so, if the wolves should eat him, we certainly would be losers!'

Jacob put his trust in God and finally gave his permission. Since Joseph trusted his brothers, he was ready to go. The very next day, they set out.

The brothers took Joseph into the wild, half-desert country, and looked for a pit to throw him into. They found a narrow well covered with two large stone-slabs. The slabs were used to prevent too much sand getting into the well when there was a wind-storm. The brothers slid the stone-slabs to one side. They took off Joseph's shirt, then bound his hands. Then they threw their brother, who had trusted them, into the well, and covered it up again. They believed they had covered up their crime. But God was a witness to what they had done.

Now they hunted for a wild goat. When they found one, they killed it. They dipped Joseph's shirt in its blood, and took it back to Jacob. By the time they reached home it was evening. When they told their story, there were tears in their eyes: 'O father, we went running races and left Joseph to look after our things. Alas! when we got back, the wolves had eaten him!'

Jacob looked at the shirt covered in blood. He held back his tears and was silent.

The brothers said: 'O but you would never believe us even when we were speaking the truth!'

Jacob looked at the shirt and he saw that it was not even torn. Wolves were supposed to have eaten his son Joseph, yet Joseph's shirt was not even torn! But Jacob did not accuse his sons. He said: 'No, indeed! But your minds have tempted you to do something . . . .'

Jacob pressed his hands against the sides of his head, to hold back his sorrow because Joseph was lost to

him. He pressed his hands against his heart to hold in the hurt because Joseph was lost to him. He turned from his sons for a moment and prayed to God and said: 'This way, lovely patience!' Peace be upon Jacob because he called for patience. Peace be upon Jacob because he called it a lovely thing.

Then Jacob said to his ten sons: 'It is in God that we must look for help, for help against what you say has happened.' After that Jacob was silent. He believed that God would restore Joseph to him in some way that he did not understand. He believed that, through Joseph, God would one day perfect His blessings upon his family. Only God knew how and where and when. Jacob must wait and keep up hope and keep up prayer.

3
Joseph is found by merchants

Joseph lay at the bottom of the well, wet and cold, and tired. When night came it was dark in the narrow well, except for a chink of light from between the stone-slabs. The light came from the stars and the moon. Joseph put his trust in God and waited for the night to pass. What hurt him most was not the cold, damp, darkness of the well, but that his own brothers had done this to him. He had given his brothers no reason for it. He asked himself: Will it ever come to light? God then answered Joseph. He assured him that, one day, he would stand before his brothers; they would not know him, but he would tell them that day how they had treated their brother.

Joseph thought of his father, Jacob, and his brother, Benjamin. How sad they must be! He prayed for God to comfort them. Very very slowly, the night passed.

Soon after first light a caravan passed nearby. They were merchants, heading for Egypt. They had been travelling by night to avoid the heat of the day. A party of them were out looking for water. One of them saw the well and let down a bucket on a rope. 'What luck!' he shouted, 'There is a young fellow here!'

Joseph was brought out of the well bedraggled and shivering with cold. He thanked them, but they did not understand. These merchants did not see the worth of Joseph. They did not try to find out who he was, or why he was in the well. They gave him some food and threw a blanket over him.

Then one of them said: 'He is not worth much, but we might get something for him in the market.' The others agreed. In case somebody passing by recognized Joseph, they wrapped him in lots of clothes and hid him with their merchandise. But God was a witness to what they did. Only when they were well clear of the area did they let Joseph out.

In the market-place in Egypt, still not realizing the worth of Joseph, they sold him for next to nothing, a handful of coins. The man who bought Joseph was an Egyptian noble, governor of the city. He had been to many markets and seen many slaves for sale. But Joseph struck him as very special. He said to himself: 'This is no ordinary young fellow! And how handsome he is!' He treated Joseph with kindness and respect.

When he arrived home, the governor said to his wife: 'Look after him, and give him a good room. He may prove to be of great use to us. Perhaps we might adopt him as our son.'

Joseph thanked God that he had been rescued from the damp, dark well and brought to so fine a place. Yet he was not free to leave, and he thought of his father and mother, and of Benjamin, and prayed for them to be comforted also.

How surprised Joseph's brothers would have been to know where he was! This is not what they had intended at all, that Joseph should be living in a fine house. But God's will cannot be prevented, and God rewards His true servants in the best way. As time passed, Joseph grew to manhood. God gave him wisdom and judgement, and Joseph became well-respected in that land.

4
A scandal against Joseph

Joseph was even more handsome as a young man than he had been as a boy. The wife of the Egyptian noble wanted him. Indeed, she wanted him so much, she could not control herself. She called Joseph into her bedroom and bolted the door. Then she commanded him to come to her bed.

Joseph did not deceive himself; he knew that he could be as weak as any man, and that he found this woman attractive. But a true servant of God cannot want to do an evil act. How kind the Egyptian noble had been to Joseph! How evil an act it would be to cheat him, as his wife wished!

So Joseph prayed to God to protect him from her. God did protect him. Joseph reminded the woman of her husband. He said to her: 'It is surely true that my master has given me a good home. It is surely true that those who do evil do not profit by it.'

Joseph had remembered God in the damp and dark well into which his jealous brothers had thrown him. He remembered God now, amid the enticing perfumes of this woman's bedroom. But the woman's thoughts were far removed from God. She was not in control

The nobles of the city realized what their wives were up to behind their backs. They feared scandal and trouble in their families on account of Joseph. So they decided to get Joseph out of the way, and they had him sent to prison. It did not matter to them that Joseph was innocent.

It mattered to Joseph. He did not want a mark on his good name. He did not want the governor of the city, who had been so kind to him, to think that perhaps he had, after all, cheated him. But Joseph put his trust in God and accepted prison.

5
Joseph explains the meaning of dreams

God made man quick-natured. He is quick to complain when things are not quite right for him. He is also quick to be unthankful and forget God. And quick when things go right for him; quick, in the midst of his happiness, to forget what he owes to God and, quick to be unthankful.

Joseph decided in his heart to remember God. He did not complain that he was in prison, although it was not just that he should be there. He was not a criminal, he had done no wrong. He said to himself: 'God has saved me from doing wrong, God has saved me from the plotting of those women. God is the best witness. God knows the truth of all things and God is just. And as God wills, He will clear my name.'

So in prison Joseph was not silent about God. Instead, he praised Him even more, and gave thanks to Him even more. He preached about God to those who would listen. In those days the people of Egypt did not pray only to God. They did not understand that the whole world and everything in it was one creation, the work of the Merciful, the One God. So, ignorant about all the powers which work in the earth and in the heavens, the people of Egypt prayed to many

different gods. They prayed to the sea and the sun, to the moon and the rivers, to the earth and to the mountains.

One day, two young men who had been put in prison on the same day as Joseph, came up to him. They said: 'We can see from your face that you are not a criminal but a man who is good and does good. We can see from your face that you are a wise man with understanding and good judgement. Can you perhaps understand the meaning of dreams?'

These men were not trying to get something out of Joseph. In prison there was nothing that Joseph could give them. So he thought: The words they have spoken are from the heart, they mean what they say. The men told Joseph their dreams.

One said: 'I dreamed that I was pressing grapes.' The second said: 'I dreamed that I was carrying bread on my head, and the birds came and pecked at it.'

Joseph said: 'Before our next meal-time comes, I will tell you the meaning of these dreams. It is the One God I serve who has given me judgement and understanding in these matters.'

Joseph paused a moment. The two men leaned forward, eager to hear. So Joseph went on:

'I have nothing to do with the religion of a people who do not believe in the One God, people who do not even believe that there is a life to come. I follow the religion of my fathers, of Abraham, of Isaac, and Jacob, upon them be peace. We do not add other gods to the One God. And that is a sign of His mercy to us and to our people.

'Tell me, my fellow-prisoners, which makes better sense: many gods quarrelling with each other, or God the One, who puts all things in order, who has power over all things? Think!

'The One God has not given us any right to invent gods, to make up names. These other gods, that is all they are, names made up by yourselves or the people who came before you.'

The two men listened patiently to what Joseph said. Then Joseph explained to them the meaning of their dreams: 'As for one of you, my fellow-prisoners, he will pour wine for a king. As for the other, he will be crucified and birds will peck at his head.'

Then Joseph said to the one who dreamed that he was pressing grapes: 'Mention me in the presence of your master.'

But when the man was freed from prison and became, in time, the king's wine-bearer, he forgot to mention Joseph to the king. Satan caused him to forget. How quick man is to forget!

But Joseph, left in prison for several years more, remembered. He remembered God and gave thanks to Him. He also remembered Jacob, his father, far away, and prayed for him to be comforted. As for Jacob, he too remembered. He pressed his hands against the side of his head, and over his heart, to hold in the hurt because his dear Joseph was lost to him, and he called on God for patience, lovely patience. Father and son alike, true believers both, were in their souls as steady as a rock, and their Lord strengthened them in their truth, and strengthened them in their belief.

The prayers of Jacob, and the prayers of Joseph, were heard and answered. For God is a witness to what goes on in a person's heart, and what God wills cannot be prevented.

6
The threads are drawn together

As God willed, the king of the Egyptians dreamed a strange dream. He could not understand its meaning. He called all his wise men and his noble councillors and told them his dream. He said: 'I saw in my dream seven fat cattle. Then seven thin and starving cattle. And the thin cattle ate up the fat ones. After that I saw seven ears of corn that were green. Then seven ears of corn that were dried up and withered.'

But the wise and noble councillors could not explain the king's dream. They did not blame themselves because they were not wise enough to understand. They blamed the dream. They said: 'It is obviously a nightmare! We know nothing about explaining nightmares!'

The king's wine-bearer overheard them, and as God willed, he remembered. After so long, he remembered Joseph. He said to the king: 'I will find out the meaning of this dream.' The king let the wine-bearer return to the prison where he told Joseph the dream.

'Joseph, you are a man of truth. Teach us the meaning of seven fat cattle eaten up by seven thin ones. Teach us the meaning of seven ears of corn all green, and seven all withered. Surely I will return to the men in the palace and, this time, surely they will know, surely they will get to hear about Joseph.'

Joseph did not accuse the wine-bearer because he had forgotten him for so long. Instead, he told him the meaning of the king's dream. He said:

'For seven years you must sow and harvest corn as you always do. But you must use up only a little of it, and put the rest in store. After those seven years will come seven very hard years. In the hard years you will use up what was laid up in store, except for a little. In this way the thin will eat up the fat. Then, after that, will come a year when the people are helped to better times; and then they will have plenty of grapes and olives to press.'

The king knew at once, as soon as he heard it, that this was the true meaning of his dream. He sent his messenger to bring Joseph out of prison.

The messenger brought the king's message, but Joseph sent him back again with another message: 'Go back to your master, and ask him to find out from the women who cut their hands. Certainly my Lord knows very well about their plotting against me.'

So the women were brought before the king of Egypt, and he questioned them. 'What were you women up to when you asked Joseph to do what you asked him to do?' The women were ashamed and they admitted

what they had done. They said: 'We know of nothing evil in him.' The governor's wife, who was also there, was ashamed and admitted what she had done. She said: 'At last the truth is uncovered. It was indeed I who caused him to be sent to prison. Indeed he is an honest and truthful man.'

Now Joseph allowed them to free him from prison. They asked him why he had not left prison when the king's messenger came to him. Joseph explained: 'It was to show you that God does not guide those who cheat. Also, it was to prove to the man who gave me a home in this land, and who was good to me, that I did not cheat him behind his back.'

Joseph's name was now cleared and he was respected in the land. He said to the people: 'There is surely something in the souls of men that pulls them to evil. So I do not say that my soul was not tempted, except that my Lord had mercy on me and saved me from myself. Indeed my Lord is perfect in forgiving, and perfect in kindness.'

The people now listened to Joseph and because of him their hearts opened a little to God. The king welcomed Joseph to his palace and favoured him. Then he put Joseph in charge of all the grain-stores of Egypt. What a relief for the people of Egypt that Joseph was in charge! The seven fat years came and the grain-stores were filled. Never had the people known a man so fair as Joseph. He set good men to watch over the workers in the fields, when they harvested and bound the corn. Joseph himself watched over his men when they weighed the grain and stored it. And God watched over them all.

In the seven years of good harvests and in the seven years of poor harvests that followed, Joseph remembered God. He also remembered his father and mother and his brothers and prayed to God to comfort them. He put his trust in God, and God was a witness to the longing in his heart to be with his own people again.

From the grain-stores that he had had filled up in the good years, Joseph shared out the grain to those who needed it. From all over Egypt people came to deal with this just man who gave in generous measure. The grain-stores of Egypt became famous far and wide, and the people came from other lands where food was scarce. They came with their merchandise to the great open courtyard where Joseph worked, and they marvelled at the goodness in this man's face. Their hearts were lightened when they traded with Joseph, for there was no-one who spoke so fairly or was so fair and honest in business.

Joseph walked amongst the different people gathered there from different lands, and he saw a group of ten men. They looked tired after their journey, but even so they seemed a strong band, almost a small army. Joseph looked at the ten men for a long time, but they did not see him. He recognized the ten men. But they did not recognize him.

7
Building for the great re-union

Joseph recognized his brothers. In his heart he felt no hate for them, he felt no anger. He wanted to go to them and say, 'Here I am, your Joseph, your long-lost brother', and take them in his arms. Joseph was a great man in Egypt and loved by the people, but still they were not his family, and Joseph longed to be united with his family. His own heart was clear. So many long years ago he had trusted them and gone with them. But they had thrown him into the well. What was in their hearts now for Joseph? Would they truly welcome him? Would they take him in their arms, truly, as brothers?

Joseph decided to find out. He walked amongst the people gathered in the courtyard and talked to them. Politely he asked after them and traded with them justly according to their means.

He came to the band of ten, and stood very close by them. How his heart went out to them in their time of need! But he held himself in control, and he did not, as he wanted to do, show himself to them. He studied the lines of their faces, so familiar, though time had changed them, and the look of their eyes, so familiar, perhaps darker now than he remembered them, as the brothers were tired from travelling.

Joseph asked about them. He asked them where they had come from, and asked about their families. How hard it was for Joseph to hold back his tears when they spoke of their aged father, Jacob! God helped Joseph, and he held himself in control. So also when they spoke of his brother Benjamin, Joseph held himself in control. But his brothers never spoke of one brother, one who was lost from the family. Joseph knew then that their hearts were still hard against him.

How could the brothers all be one family again? If Joseph called his father and mother and his brother Benjamin, they would surely come to him. But the ten would not come, they would stay away, and the family would be broken? How could he mend their hearts and bring them all together? Joseph decided on a plan.

Joseph gave his brothers all that they had come for, and more, and took in exchange the few goods they had brought to trade. He said to them: 'Next time, bring your other brother with you, bring him to me from your father.' When they were silent, and Joseph knew and God knew why they were silent, Joseph said: 'You see what generous measures I have given to you. Have I not been a good host to you? But I tell you, if you do not bring your brother to me, there will be no measure for you next time, nor will I receive you.'

The brothers hung their heads. They said: 'We will ask our father. That much we can do.' They knew that their father would refuse.

But Joseph also knew it. He told the men who worked for him to go in secret and put all the goods the brothers had brought with them back into their saddle-bags. He said: 'They will find out when they get home to their people. Then, may be, they will return.'

The brothers reached their people and went to Jacob and they told him what the guardian of the grain-stores of Egypt had said. They told him they must take Benjamin with them next time, or they would be refused. They pleaded with Jacob and said: 'Surely we will be watching over him.' Jacob remembered those words, and the sorrow rose in his heart for the son who was lost to him. He said: 'If I trust him to you, how would it be different from when I trusted his brother to you before? No, but God is the best guardian and protector. Out of all those who show mercy, God is the most merciful.'

The brothers saw that they could not change his mind. It hurt them that their father did not trust them, but in their hearts they knew that they did not deserve to be trusted. Then they opened their saddle-bags and found all their goods. They said to Jacob: 'Look, all our goods have been sent back with us! What more could we ask for? If we go again we will get all the food we need for our family, and a lot more, and we will watch over our brother.'

How wisely Joseph had judged! Jacob saw that he must let Benjamin go, for his family's sake, and because in Egypt he would be received by a man who was good. Indeed he must be good, this man in Egypt, because he had returned to his sons all their merchandise.

Jacob put his trust in God, and said to his ten sons: 'I will never send him with you unless you make a promise by God to bring him back to me safe and sound, unless it happens that you are under attack and have no choice.' The brothers made this promise and God was a witness over them while they made it.

Certainly the brothers meant to look after Benjamin. When they threw Joseph down the well, they had wanted to be closer in their father's favour. But it had not brought them closer. With Joseph out of the way, they had hoped Jacob would forget Joseph and prefer them. But this had not happened either. He remembered Joseph all the more, and so loved and missed him that his tears had weakened his eyes. Truly, they did not want to add to their father's sorrow.

As for Joseph, their hearts were still set against him. They did not yet understand why Jacob had preferred Joseph, and not them. But the reason was there in their hearts. It was only that they could not see it.

When, as God willed, the time came for them to return to Egypt, Jacob said to them: 'O my sons, do not enter by the same gate. Enter by separate gates.' Jacob knew that what God willed could not be prevented. He said: 'But I cannot advise you in any way that will help you against God. God alone is the best judge of what happens. I have put my trust in Him. And everyone who puts their trust should put their trust in God.'

As they travelled, the brothers thought about Jacob's words. After a time they understood them. They understood that they should not put their trust in their plots, thinking they could get round God's will. Certainly their plot against Joseph had not worked. So the ten put their trust in God, and watched over Benjamin. They thought to themselves, indeed this is how we should have looked after Joseph the last time.

When they reached the city in Egypt, they entered separately by different gates. Joseph was able to find Benjamin by himself without the others. He told him who he was, and they clung to each other. Joseph told Benjamin all that had happened. Then he explained to Benjamin how he meant to win back the love of his brothers, and make them all one family. Benjamin understood and again the brothers embraced, and what tears of joy they each shed.

Benjamin rejoined the ten brothers where they had agreed to meet, in the great courtyard. There Joseph came out to them, and he received them as he had promised to receive them, and gave them the fullest measure of what they needed for their families. They were well-pleased, and still watching over Benjamin, they loaded up their camels and set off on their way home.

Before they left, Joseph had told one of his men to hide a valuable cup in the saddle-bag of his brother Benjamin. When the brothers' caravan was a little way out of the city, he sent messengers after them on horseback. Then he himself followed a little later.

The messengers caught up with the caravan, and said: 'Stop! You are thieves!' The brothers were astonished. They asked: 'Why, what is it that you are missing?' The messengers said: 'We are missing the king's cup. Whoever finds it gets a full camel-load in reward.'

'By God!' said the brothers. 'You know very well that we are not thieves, nor did we come to make trouble in the land!'

'Oh,' said the messengers, 'and how will you make up for it if the cup is found in one of your saddle-bags?'

The brothers were confident that the cup would not be found among their things. They answered according to the law of Abraham, their great ancestor. They said: 'The very person in whose bags it is found, he will make up for it.'

Of course the cup was found among the things in Benjamin's saddle-bag. Benjamin was seized.

The ten brothers were upset. The grudge, deep in their hearts, against Joseph rose again. They did not want to be linked with Joseph as brothers. They still did not recognize this man as Joseph, and when he took hold of Benjamin, they said angrily: 'If he is a thief, a brother of his was a thief before.'

How could they tell such a lie against Joseph? But Joseph said nothing to them. He was sad that in their hearts they were still against him. He thought to himself: You call me a thief unjustly; though what you have done is worse. God knows very well the truth of what you are saying.

God then rewarded Joseph's trust in Him, for his brothers said: 'O exalted one, we see that you are a man who does good. Take one of us in his place, we beg you; he has a father who is very old.'

Here was proof that Joseph's brothers cared at least for his father, Jacob, and for his brother, Benjamin. They were ready to be taken in Benjamin's place; they were willing to do everything to honour their promise to Jacob. But still there was a grudge in their hearts against Joseph, so Joseph knew he must wait. He said: 'We cannot take any person except the one in whose things the stolen cup was found. If we did that, we would be wrong-doers.' The brothers tried to change Joseph's mind, but they could not. After all, it was according to the law of their own people that Benjamin was seized.

They talked amongst themselves. The eldest said he was too ashamed to return to Jacob without Benjamin. 'I will never leave this land until my father gives me permission, or God judges in my favour. God is the best of judges.'

At last, the hearts of these men were turning to God. Soon, they would be one united family again, a strong band because they all trusted equally in God.

8
The re-union

The eldest brother would not leave with the others. He said to them: 'Return the rest of you. Say to our father: "Father, your son stole; we are not saying anything except what we know to be so. We couldn't have known what was going to happen, we are not guardians of the Unseen." Then say to him: "Ask in the city we were in, ask the others in the caravan which went with us. They will bear us out, we are truthful men!"'

So nine of his sons came back to Jacob, instead of eleven. They said what the eldest had told them to say. Jacob answered: 'No, but your minds have tempted you to do something. This way, lovely patience!'

The nine sons who heard their father say this were innocent this time; they had been guilty the time before. Again they watched as their father pressed his hands to the sides of his head and to his heart, to hold in the hurt. His hands were showing the way to patience, calling it to him: 'This way, lovely patience!' The nine sons were nearly heart-broken, but they held back their tears, ashamed before the old man.

Then Jacob said: 'It may be God will bring them all back to me. God is the One who knows, and He alone is wise.' He turned away from them and said, for it was not for them to hear: 'Alas, alas, my Joseph!'

But his sons heard him. They wanted to comfort him in his great sorrow. They said: 'By God, you will never give up remembering Joseph until you have pined right away or until you are among the dying!' They wanted to comfort him, but how could they comfort him unless they admitted what they had done with Joseph? They saw their father's eyes were full of the sorrow that he had held in for so long.

Jacob was blind now, but he knew from God what his sons did not. He knew that through Joseph, God's blessing on his family, the family of Jacob, would be perfected. Somehow, Joseph would be restored to him. Afraid that, unlike himself, his nine sons were near to losing hope for his family, he commanded them to go out in search of Joseph and his brother. He said to them: 'Do not give up hope of God's comfort; no man gives up that hope unless he is one of the unbelievers.'

The nine brothers travelled again to Egypt and joined their eldest, and they came, all ten together into the presence of Joseph. Joseph looked at them. How changed they were! Surely now, now it was time to make himself known to them. Still, he waited to hear what they would say.

They spoke of the sorrow of Jacob, and they spoke of his blindness. 'O exalted one, trouble has come to our people. We have very little this time, and the little we have is not worth much. Even so, be kind to us. Surely God rewards those who are kind.'

Joseph thought: How humbly and movingly they speak, now! He asked them: 'Do you understand now how you behaved with Joseph and his brother, when you behaved like those who do not know God?'

The brothers looked, and looked again more closely. They recognized Joseph. There was no need to answer his question because, of all people, Joseph knew best what they had done, and their sadness about it was on their faces. They said softly: 'Are you truly Joseph?' He answered just as softly: 'I am Joseph, and this Benjamin is my brother!' At last the brothers could take one another in their arms, all twelve together, and none held back his tears.

Joseph said: 'God has been kind to us. Whoever fears God and holds firm, God does not throw away the reward of those who do good.'

The ten said: 'By God, it is true that God has preferred you over us, and it is true that we did wrong.'

Joseph answered them: 'No. No word of blame on this day. God will forgive you. Out of all those who show mercy, God is the most merciful.'

Then Joseph brought a shirt of his and said to them: 'Go now and take this to my father, and lay it over his eyes, and his sight will return to him. After that bring all the family here together.'

9
The dream comes true

Even before the caravan had reached Jacob's land, Jacob felt something on the air. He called to the people around him and said to them: 'I can sense the scent of Joseph on the air. Though you may think I am in my silly old age.' Those around him said: 'That's certainly the case.'

But when the caravan came, how Jacob was rewarded, for his hope and his trust in God, for his lovely patience. When Joseph's shirt was laid over his eyes, his sight at once came back to him. He thanked God with all the might of his great soul, and said to his sons: 'How often I told you that I knew from God what you did not know!' The ten called on their father to pray to God and ask forgiveness for them for their crimes. Jacob said: 'I will certainly ask my Lord to forgive you. He is the Forgiver, the Merciful.'

The family of Jacob entered Egypt together, and they entered the city together, a strong band. Joseph received his parents with tenderness, welcoming them, as God willed, to a secure life. He led them to the dining hall in his great house, and seated them in the part that was raised up above the rest. He seated his eleven brothers together in the other part. Before the meal all of them together bowed to Joseph, who said:

'Look, father, here is the meaning of my dream. God, my Lord, has made it true!'

The sun and moon in the dream meant Joseph's father and mother, and the eleven stars meant his brothers. Now he was indeed set in authority over them.

Joseph praised God for His blessings upon the family of Jacob. Satan had come between him and his brothers for a time. But God had more than forgiven his brothers' wrong. It seemed that the wrong had been undone, all their sorrows had passed away, and their wounds all healed.

Joseph turned to God in prayer. He said:

'O my Lord, it is You who have given me a measure of power in this land, and You who have shown me how to understand the inner meaning of events. O Creator of the heavens and the earth, You are my defender in this life and the life to come. Welcome me to Yourself as Your true servant, and join me with those who do good.'

Peace be upon Joseph for his wisdom and judgement.

Peace be upon Joseph for his trust in God, and for his patience, and for his forgiving heart.